Date: 3/15/12

J 579 OWE
Owen, Ruth,
Creepy backyard invaders /

Up Close and GROSS
Microscopic Creatures

CREEPY
BACKYARD INVADERS

by Ruth Owen

Consultant: Suzy Gazlay, M.A.
Recipient, Presidential Award
for Excellence in Science Teaching

BEARPORT
PUBLISHING

New York, New York

Credits

Cover and title page, © Clouds Hill Imaging/www.lastrefuge.co.uk; 3, © Clouds Hill Imaging/www.lastrefuge.co.uk; 4, © Power and Syred/Science Photo Library; 5, © Clouds Hill Imaging/www.lastrefuge.co.uk; 6, © Tom Oates/Wikipedia (public domain); 7, © Power and Syred/Science Photo Library; 8, © Konrad Wothe/Minden Pictures/ FLPA; 9T, © Ted Kinsman/Science Photo Library; 9B © Science Faction/Superstock; 10, © Nigel Cattlin/Science Photo Library; 11, © Clouds Hill Imaging/www.lastrefuge.co.uk; 12, © Volker Steger/Science Photo Library; 13, © Clouds Hill Imaging/www.lastrefuge. co.uk; 14, © Nigel Cattlin/FLPA; 15, © Clouds Hill Imaging/www.lastrefuge.co.uk; 16, © Martin Dohrn/Science Photo Library; 17, © Clouds Hill Imaging/www.lastrefuge.co.uk; 18, © Mitsuhiko Imamori/Minden Pictures/FLPA; 19T, © Chris Howey/Shutterstock; 19B, © Clouds Hill Imaging/www.lastrefuge.co.uk; 20T, © Shutterstock; 20B, © Food and Drink/Superstock; 21, © Clouds Hill Imaging/www.lastrefuge.co.uk; 22T, © Scott Bauer/US Department of Agriculture/Science Photo Library; 22C, © Clouds Hill Imaging/www.lastrefuge.co.uk; 22B, © Clouds Hill Imaging/www.lastrefuge.co.uk.

Publisher: Kenn Goin
Senior Editor: Lisa Wiseman
Creative Director: Spencer Brinker
Design: Alix Wood
Photo Researcher: Ruby Tuesday Books Ltd

Library of Congress Cataloging-in-Publication Data

Owen, Ruth, 1967–
 Creepy backyard invaders / by Ruth Owen.
 p. cm. —(Up close and gross: microscopic creatures)
 Includes bibliographical references and index.
 ISBN-13: 978-1-61772-125-0 (library binding)
 ISBN-10: 1-61772-125-5 (library binding)
 1. Microorganisms—Juvenile literature. 2. Microbiology—Juvenile literature. I.
Title.
 QR57.O94 2011
 579—dc22

                                2010041212

Published in the United States of America by Bearport Publishing Company, Inc.

For more information, write to Bearport Publishing Company, Inc., 101 Fifth Avenue, Suite 6R, New York, New York 10003. Printed in the United States of America in North Mankato, Minnesota.

121510
10810CGB

10 9 8 7 6 5 4 3 2 1

Contents

Who's Living in Your Backyard?

A backyard is often home to birds, frogs, and squirrels. These backyard creatures are big enough to see easily. However, it's much harder to spot the millions of tiny spiders and insects, such as whiteflies and ladybugs, that are hunting, raising their young, and even going to war with one another in every corner of a person's backyard.

In this book you will have a chance to see amazing images of tiny backyard invaders. Using powerful **microscopes**, scientists have zoomed in on these living things to show them up close and in great detail. So get ready to be amazed by the tiny invaders that share your backyard. Just watch where you step!

This ladybug is about to land on a flower. Its white flight wings are protected by its hard red outer wings.

A whitefly looks like a tiny white dot when you see it with just your eyes. However, if you take a look at this insect under a microscope, you will see a creature that looks like an alien from another planet!

This creature is shown **150 TIMES** its actual size!

Mouthparts

Whiteflies use their mouthparts to suck juices from the stems of plants. This damages the plants.

Earwig Super-Moms

During the day, earwigs rest under stones or rotting logs and leaves. At night, these tiny insect invaders search for food such as other insects, dead animals, and rotting plants.

Unlike most insects, earwigs take care of their eggs and young. Female earwigs lay their eggs in damp places. This keeps them from drying out, which would hurt the young earwigs developing inside. If the eggs start to get dry, the mother moves them to a new damp place. She also uses her mouthparts to clean and turn her eggs. This keeps **mold** from growing on them. The mother guards her eggs from centipedes, daddy longlegs, and other **predators**. When the young, called **nymphs**, hatch she continues to guard them until they are old enough to defend themselves.

Nymph

Egg

Female earwig

A female earwig protecting her eggs and nymphs

Pincers

Rotting leaf

Earwigs use body parts called pincers to grab food and defend themselves against predators.

People once thought earwigs climbed into their ears at night and laid eggs in their brains. That is how earwigs got their name. Thankfully, this old story isn't true!

7

Helpful Honeybees

Honeybees are important backyard invaders that help plants **reproduce**. Plants make new plants by growing seeds inside of them. To do so, a plant must be **pollinated**. This happens when a yellow dust called **pollen** is moved from the male part of a plant's flower to the female part. Pollen can be moved by animals or even the wind.

When a honeybee lands on a flower, pollen sticks to its furry body. As it walks around inside the flower, the bee moves pollen from the male part of the flower to the female part. Flowers get honeybees to visit them by making pollen and a sweet liquid called **nectar**, which the bees love to eat.

This honeybee is covered with pollen inside of a pumpkin flower.

People should try not to harm honeybees because they may sting in self-defense. When a bee stings someone, it pushes its stinger into a person's skin. Then, as the bee tries to fly away, its stinger is ripped from its body along with some of its insides. As a result, the bee dies.

Stinger

A honeybee about to sting a person

Some of the bee's insides

Stinger

This is a honeybee's stinger and some of its insides that have been ripped from the bee's body.

Attack of the Plant-Sucking Aphids

Aphids are tiny insects that feed on juice from plants. This juice, called **sap**, carries water and **nutrients** through a plant. The aphids use their sharp mouthparts to pierce the plant's stem and suck up the sap. If the aphids suck up too much sap, it can kill a plant.

Inside an aphid, sap is turned into a waste product called **honeydew**. The aphid releases this sweet liquid waste out of an opening on its bottom. Honeydew might be aphid waste, but ants love to eat it! Ants will even protect aphids from predators such as ladybugs to make sure they get their supply of honeydew.

Aphids

An ant defends a group of tiny green aphids from an attack by a ladybug.

Sometimes aphids suck all the sap out of a plant. When this happens, ants will carry the aphids to a new plant so they can make more honeydew!

Sharp mouthparts

Aphids can be green, white, black, yellow, and even pink. Here, a black aphid sucks sap from a plant stem.

Life in an Ant Colony

Ants are insects that live in huge groups called **colonies**. Most types of ants make their homes in underground nests that they build. Inside a colony's nest, one of the female ants, called the queen, lays eggs. Other female ants, called workers, then care for the eggs and the young. The worker ants also look for food, such as other insects, fruit, and scraps left by humans, to feed the colony.

Ants sometimes enter houses looking for food. If they find food left out on a countertop uncovered, they will take some of it back to the other ants. As they head back to the nest, they leave a **scent trail**. The trail leads from the food inside the house back to the nest. Soon, hundreds of workers will be following the trail back and forth, collecting more food.

Jaws

Antenna

This photo shows two ants fighting. One ant has grabbed the other's antenna in its jaws.

Sometimes an ant colony attacks another colony. The attackers may steal the other colony's eggs and young to eat. The ants under attack will fight to the death to protect their nest.

Brown sugar

An ant looking for food climbs into a bowl of brown sugar.

Lacewings, the Gardener's Friend

Many gardeners welcome lacewings, a type of insect, into their backyards. The reason is that the lacewing's worm-like young, called **larvae**, eat backyard pests such as aphids that often kill plants. Some types of adult lacewings also eat aphids, but they mostly feed on pollen, nectar, and honeydew.

Female lacewings lay their eggs under leaves in places where there are many aphids to eat. Each tiny egg is attached to one end of a hair-like strand of **silk**. The silk is made inside the female's body and quickly hardens once it's released. The other end of the strand is attached to a leaf. The silk strands hold the eggs away from the leaf, keeping them safe. Predators such as ants are too heavy to walk along the silk strands to attack the eggs.

The silk strands of the lacewing eggs are very short—less than ¼ inch (6 mm) long.

Lacewing larvae have long, curved mouthparts that they use to pierce their prey's body. Then they suck the body dry of all its juices.

An adult lacewing's body is about half an inch (1.3 cm) long.

This creature is shown **55 TIMES** its actual size!

aphid —

— larva

A lacewing larva holds an aphid in its curved mouthparts.

Daredevil Jumping Spiders

Jumping spiders are predators that leap great distances to **pounce** on their prey. Before it jumps, the spider releases a silk safety line from inside its body and attaches it to a starting place. If the spider misses its landing spot, it can climb back up the safety line.

A jumping spider has eight eyes to help it spot prey. Its two big, front-facing eyes give it stereoscopic vision. This means the spider sees the same picture with both its eyes, just as humans do. Having stereoscopic vision helps the spider figure out how far away something is. That's very important for chasing and pouncing on prey.

Safety line

A jumping spider about to pounce on a cricket

Some types of jumping spiders can jump up to 40 times their own length. That's like an adult human jumping the length of two and a half basketball courts!

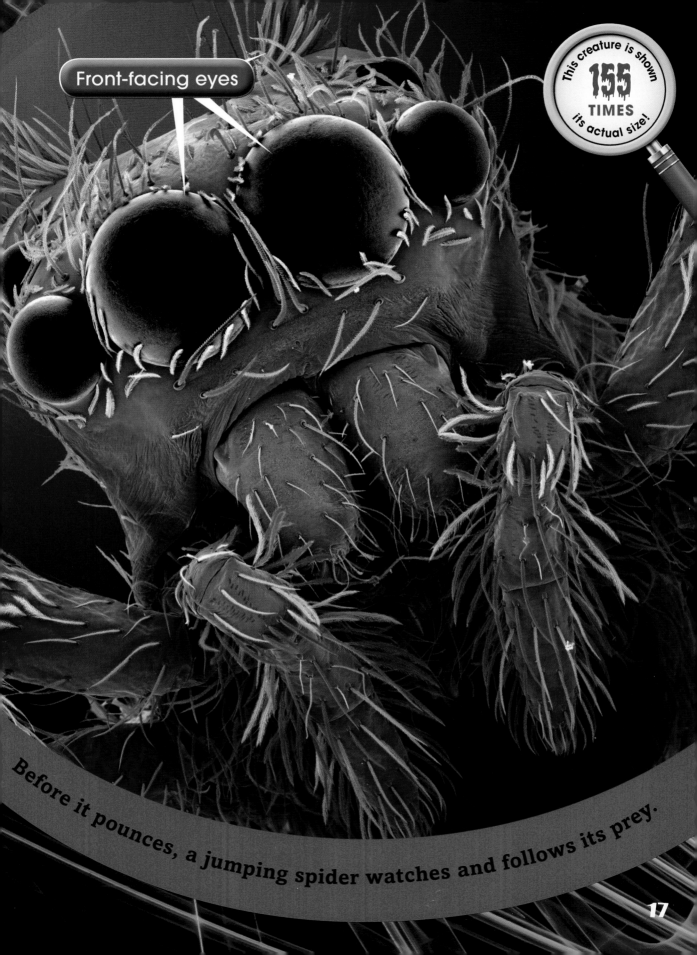

Front-facing eyes

Before it pounces, a jumping spider watches and follows its prey.

Roly-Poly Woodlice

Lift up a rock or a rotting log in a backyard, and woodlice will crawl away in all directions! These little creatures may look like insects, but they're not. They are **crustaceans**, a group of animals that also includes crabs and shrimp. Woodlice live in damp places and feed on dead, rotting plants.

Like other crustaceans, woodlice have a hard outer covering called an **exoskeleton**. The exoskeleton is made up of many different sections that slightly overlap. The sections allow woodlice to bend and curve their armored bodies. Some types of woodlice can roll into a tight ball. They do this to protect themselves when threatened by a predator.

Young woodlouse

Young woodlice look like tiny white versions of their mother.

Female woodlice carry their eggs in a liquid-filled pouch under their bodies. When the young woodlice hatch from the eggs, they crawl out of the pouch.

A woodlouse rolling
into a ball

Exoskeleton

People have given woodlice lots of names such as
"pill bugs" and "roly-polys."

Stinging Nettles

Some backyard invaders are plants. Stinging nettles are a kind of plant that grow in the countryside and among weeds in people's backyards. Many types of insects feed on stinging nettles, but for humans they can be a painful backyard invader!

The leaves and stems of stinging nettles are covered with tiny hairs that have sharp points. If a person touches these hairs, even lightly, they will break off and pierce the skin. As a hair enters the skin, a mixture of stinging chemicals is released. A nettle sting is very painful and itchy, but it doesn't cause any lasting damage.

Stinging nettles

For hundreds of years, people have used stinging nettles in their food. The nettles can be boiled to make soup and tea. In Cornwall, England, Yarg cheese is wrapped in nettles to give it a dark green outer skin, called a rind.

Cornish Yarg cheese wrapped in stinging

Sharp hair

The stinging chemicals are stored here.

The hairs on the stem of a stinging nettle are the plant's defense against large animals, such as cattle, that will try to eat it.

Getting Up Close

The amazing close-up photographs in this book were created using a very powerful microscope. It is called a scanning **electron** microscope, or SEM.

Microscopes make things look bigger. A scanning electron microscope can show what things look like hundreds of times their real size.

How were the photos in this book created?

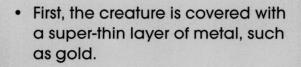

- First, the creature is covered with a super-thin layer of metal, such as gold.

- Next, the SEM passes a beam of tiny particles called electrons over the creature. The electrons bounce off the metal around the creature and create electrical signals. These signals are turned into a black-and-white image of the creature on a computer.

- Scientists then add color to the SEM image using a computer.

Glossary

colonies (KOL-uh-neez) large groups of related insects that are all the offspring of the same queens

crustaceans (kruhss-TAY-shuhnz) groups of animals, such as lobsters or shrimp, that have hard outer skeletons and jointed legs

electron (i-LEK-tron) a tiny particle that is found in atoms, the building blocks of all matter; electrons carry electrical charges

exoskeleton (*eks*-oh-SKEL-uh-tuhn) the hard outer covering that protects the bodies of some kinds of animals, such as insects, spiders, and crustaceans

honeydew (HUHN-ee-doo) a sweet liquid released by aphids that ants and other insects may eat

larvae (LAR-vee) the worm-like form of many young insects; singular form is *larva*

microscopes (MYE-kruh-skohps) tools used to see things that are too small to see with the eyes alone

mold (MOHLD) a furry fungus that grows on the surface of damp or rotting plants, animal matter, or food

nectar (NEK-tur) a sugary liquid produced by plants that attracts bees and other animals that transfer pollen from one part of a plant to another

nutrients (NOO-tree-uhnts) things that are found in food and are needed by people and animals to stay healthy

nymphs (NIMFS) the young of some types of insects, such as earwigs

pollen (POL-uhn) tiny yellow grains that are part of a plant's process of reproduction

pollinated (POL-uh-*nayt*-id) when pollen is carried from the male part of a flower to the female part; pollen can be moved to flowers on the same plant or to a different plant

pounce (POUNSS) to jump onto something suddenly

predators (PRED-uh-turz) animals that hunt and kill other animals for food

reproduce (*ree*-pruh-DOOSS) to produce more of a living thing, such as an animal or a plant

sap (SAP) a liquid that carries water and nutrients through a plant

scent trail (SENT TRAYL) an invisible scented path left behind by an animal or person

silk (SILK) a soft, shiny, thread-like substance that is made by some insects and spiders

Index

Bibliography

BBC Science and Nature: www.bbc.co.uk/sn/

Warren, Adrian. *Unseen Companions.* Wells, Somerset, UK: Last Refuge Ltd. (2007).

Read More

Goldish, Meish. *Jumping Spiders (No Backbone!).* New York: Bearport (2009).

Johnson, Jinny. *Simon & Schuster Children's Guide to Insects and Spiders.* New York: Simon & Schuster Children's Publishing (1997).

Llewellyn, Claire. *The Best Book of Bugs.* Boston: Kingfisher (2005).

Lovett, Sarah. *Extremely Weird Micro Monsters.* Santa Fe, NM: John Muir Publications (1996).

Learn More Online

To learn more about backyard invaders, visit
www.bearportpublishing.com/UpCloseandGross

About The Author

Ruth Owen has been writing children's books for more than ten years.
She lives in Cornwall, England, just minutes from the ocean.
Ruth loves gardening and caring for her family of llamas.